Under God's Grace

Journal

Tomeko Brown
Illustrations Christopher Smallwood

TO:

_____

FROM:

_____

GIVEN TO ME:

_____

The Temple

The Temple is where I want to be
To feel His presence all over me
A preached Word
That overrides the fear inside of me
It's in the Temple you will find
The presence of His Divine
It's in His Temple you will receive
Forgiveness, Rebirth, and Strength to proceed

Nobody but Jesus

No One could have done it
Felt the pain like He did
Hung and Bleed on the Cross
Suffered for our many sins
No one could have done it
Died and Rose again
No one could have done it
Nobody but Jesus
Now open and let Him come in

To Know Him

To know Him
Is Peace
To know Him
Is Joy
To know Him
Is Wisdom
To know Him
Is to have so much more
To know Him
How true
To Know Him
And have Him live within you

The Twelve

Ordinary men
With different challenges they faced
Fisherman, Tax Collector
All needing God's Grace
Living lives like you and I
Giving an opportunity other than just to get by
The Twelve He chose to walk along side with
Him
So open your eyes
Do you see?
These Twelve were just like you and me
So what's holding you back from taking that
step
Answer the call
Live a life you will never regret

Running Strong

I'm running strong again
God gave me new wings
Tested and tried
This fear needed to subside
Got my mind back
Body going strong
Just like David
He created a new heart in me
Now I can see clearly
A new vision
Old things behind me
Chasing His will
He has placed before me
To soar high like the birds in the sky
I can't give in now
Old things I say...Bye-Bye

An Open Door

Knock, Knock
Open Up
And open door that no one can shut
Goals, dreams, all in between
Why want this door open
Waiting long, waiting patiently
Open Up
Is anyone listening
A giant "Sigh"
I begin to wonder
Shattered dreams, broken promises
Pushed to the limited
Tried to hard
But wait a minute
In due time
Open Up
And it will be what's mine

www.ingramcontent.com/pod-product-compliance
Lightning Source LLC
Chambersburg PA
CBHW060651150426
42813CB00052B/589